The Whole30 Crockpot Cookbook

87 Quick, Easy and Delicious Recipes for Your Crock Pot Express Pressure Cooker

Carmela Madison

© Copyright 2020 by Carmela Madison - All rights reserved.

This document is geared towards providing exact and reliable information in regards to the topic and issue covered. The publication is sold with the idea that the publisher is not required to render accounting, officially permitted, or otherwise, qualified services. If advice is necessary, legal or professional, a practiced individual in the profession should be ordered.

From a Declaration of Principles which was accepted and approved equally by a Committee of the American Bar Association and a Committee of Publishers and Associations.

In no way is it legal to reproduce, duplicate, or transmit any part of this document in either electronic means or in printed format. Recording of this publication is strictly prohibited and any storage of this document is not allowed unless with written permission from the publisher. All rights reserved.

The information provided herein is stated to be truthful and consistent, in that any liability, in terms of inattention or otherwise, by any usage or abuse of any policies, processes, or directions contained within is the solitary and utter responsibility of the recipient reader. Under no circumstances will any legal responsibility or blame be held against the publisher for any reparation, damages, or monetary loss due to the information herein, either directly or indirectly.

Respective authors own all copyrights not held by the publisher.

CONTENTS

Introduction 7
What are the Whole30 Foods? 7
The Health Benefits of the Whole30 Diet 8
The Whole30 Diet Rules 10

Introduction to Crock-Pot 13
The Benefits of Using a Crock-Pot 13
What are Some Tips on How to Best Use My Crock-Pot? 15

Whole30 Crock-Pot Meat Recipes 19
Crock-Pot Turkey Breast 19
Crock-Pot Orange Chicken 20
Whole30 Savory Tater Tot 21
Whole30 Chili Lime Turkey 22
Whole30 Beef and Cabbage Stew 23
Crock-Pot Beef Steak 24
Whole30 Colorful Lamb 25
Crock-Pot Irish Stew 26
Crock-Pot Special Leg of Lamb 27
Crock-Pot Jamaican Jerk Pork Roast 28
Herbed Carrots Pork 29
Crock-Pot Beef Brisket 31
Whole Roasted Chicken 32
Crock-Pot Turkey Meatballs 33
Whole30 Pork Carnitas 34

Whole30 Crock-Pot Seafood Recipes 35

Crock-Pot Scallion Salmon..........................35
Whole30 Crock-Pot Cod Curry 36
Whole30 Tangy Cod Fillets..........................37
Rosemary Cod Fillets 38
Crock-Pot Energetic Salmon Fillets 39
Whole30 Foolproof Mahi-Mahi Fillets 40
Crock-Pot Whole30 Cauliflower Fish................41
Crock-Pot Super Easy Mahi-Mahi 42
Crock-Pot Quick Lobster 43
Crock-Pot Salmon with Vegetables 44
Whole30 Lemon Salmon.............................45
Crock-Pot Moroccan Fish 46
Crock-Pot Mahi-Mahi with Carrots..................48
Crock-Pot Fish Curry.................................49
Crock-Pot Delicious Mussels........................50

Whole30 Crock-Pot Soup Recipes............... 53

Crock-Pot Mexican Beef Soup 53
Whole30 Crock-Pot Chicken Veggie Soup 54
Crock-Pot Vegetable Pork Soup 55
Whole30 Veggie Soup................................56
Crock-Pot Green Soup 57
Whole30 Zucchini Ginger Soup.....................58
Crock-Pot Savory Carrot Soup 59
Crock-Pot Turkey Thai Soup 60
Crock-Pot Curried Broccoli Soup....................61
Crock-Pot Special Chicken Soup 63
Crock-Pot Chicken Tortilla Whole30 Soup 64
Crock-Pot Yummy Lamb Soup......................66

Whole30 Vegetable Turkey Soup 67
Crock-Pot Omega-3 Salmon Soup 68
Whole30 Red Curry Soup 69

Whole30 Crock-Pot Desserts and Snacks Recipes 71

Crock-Pot Chicken Wings............................. 71
Crock-Pot Spiced Nuts 72
Crock-Pot Whole30 Nut Porridge 73
Crock-Pot Cajun Spiced Pecans 74
Crock-Pot Butternut Squash 75
Crock-Pot Roasted Spicy Olives 76
Crock-Pot Baked Potatoes 77
Crock-Pot Garlic Lemon Scallops 78
Whole30 Cooked Guacamole......................... 79
Pumpkin Butter 80
Crock-Pot Whole30 Applesauce 81
Crock-Pot Almond Butter Banana 82
Crock-Pot Grain Free Berry Cobbler 83
Spinach Mushroom Treat............................. 84
Crock-Pot Apple Butter................................ 85
Crock-Pot Stuffed Apples with Figs 86
Whole30 Crock-Pot Apple Cinnamon Quinoa 87

Whole30 Crock-Pot Appetizer Recipes 89

Crock-Pot Buffalo Wings.............................. 89
Crock-Pot Avocado Wedges 90
Crock-Pot Spicy Pickles 91
Whole30 Sweet Potato Bacon Tots................. 92

Crock-Pot Carrot Fries 93
Whole30 Brussels Sprouts with Bacon Garlic Aioli
.... 94
Bacon Compote and Caramelized Onion on Sweet
Potato 96
Crock-Pot Whole30 Zucchini 97
Whole30 Cobb-Style Potato 98
Whole30 Teriyaki Poppers 99

Whole30 Crock-Pot Beverages Recipes 101

Whole30 Berry Kombucha Beverage 101
Crock-Pot Berry Lemonade Tea 102
Whole30 Red Cherry Cider 103
Crock-Pot Spiced Peachy Cider 104
Crock-Pot Red Hot Punch 105
Crock-Pot Spiced Pear Cider 106
Crock-Pot Spiked Cider 107
Crock-Pot Spiced Apple Orange Cider 108
Whole30 Swedish Glögg 109
Whole30 Homemade Lemonade 110
Crock-Pot Hot Pomegranate Punch 111
Whole30 Fruit Punch 112
Ginger Lemon Tea 113
Whole30 Hot Mulled Cider 114
Crock-Pot Ginger Spiced Cider 115

Conclusion 117

Introduction

The whole30 diet was founded by Melissa and Dallas Hartwig in 2009. Whole30 is a 30 days diet and a short-term nutrition reset that can fundamentally change your relationship with food and lead to a healthier lifestyle. The only thing you have to do is to say lot of "Nos", no carbs, no beans, no dairy and no eggs. It is much like the Paleo diet in which you eliminate all the foods that can be hunted or gathered. Due to the whole30 program, the body is healed from the damages that might be caused by consuming foods that irritate the gut.

What are the Whole30 Foods?

Eating real food is emphasized by whole30. The majority of the Western diet is comprised of the industrialized foods which are strictly prohibited in the whole30 program. The whole30 diet comprises of only meat, seeds, nuts, oils, ghee, fruits and vegetables. Since the diet comprises of all-natural foods, you will ultimately have to forget all artificial and unhealthy foods to help you recuperate a healthy life ahead. The starchy nutrient-dense vegetables, like potatoes and sweet potatoes (can only be taken if the person exercises regularly), refined and unrefined added sugar, legumes, processed foods, dairy (ghee is an exception), bakery items, MSG, sulfates and alcohol are forbidden to eat during whole30 diet.

The Health Benefits of the Whole30 Diet

There are lots and lots of benefits of whole food diet, the major benefits include following.

1. Better Digestion System

When you are on whole30 diet, you will feel that your digestion system is working better than ever by eating natural foods.

2. Controlled Sugar Levels

As the whole30 diet does not consist of any added sugars, so the sugar level will be in control and many other internal problems will be solved.

3. Healthier Lifestyle

With the help of whole30 diet, you will achieve the healthier lifestyle that you have always dreamt about. You will find it astonishingly startling with the great and unusual taste of foods.

4. High Energy Level

Due to your improved digestive system, your energy level will boost for daily routine.

5. Enhanced Immunity

One of the major benefits of whole30 diet is that a protection shield is developed against the diseases by you. Your immunity system becomes strong.

6. Glowing Skin

By following the whole30 diet plan, you will feel that your skin has become fresh and has started glowing like a shining star. This is because you have stopped eating toxins from fattening and unhealthy processed foods.

7. Relieved Muscular Pains

Due to the whole30 foods, your muscles will become strong and all sorts of muscular pains will be relieved.

8. Weight Loss

The major reason that most of the people accept the whole30 challenge is to lose weight. It is known as a weight loss diet because it lacks gluten, fattening processed foods, dairy and sugar, and comprises of all the healthy ingredients. So, if you want to lose weight in healthy manner and with more permanent results, then you must count on this diet.

9. Attainment of Satisfaction

The best and the most favorite benefit of the whole30 diet are the contentment and satisfaction you attain by becoming the chef of the family. It feels a good deal of pleasure to cook all the food yourself. You don't need to worry, as all the recipes in this book are very easy and you can prepare them quickly with least amount of time.

The Whole30 Diet Rules

For those of you, who are taking this life-changing challenge and thinking how hard it might be to stay strict on this diet, certain rules have been devised. These rules will provide you motivation to stick to the plan for the whole month even when there are many hurdles and distractions.

1. Eat Real Food

You have to eat moderate amount of seafood, eggs and meat; some fruits; vegetables; natural fats; and spices, herbs and seasonings. Just make your habit to eat foods with fewer ingredients.

2. Avoid Certain Foods

Say no to alcohol, added sugars, legumes, grains, MSG, sulphites, dairy products, junk food and baked goods.

3. Do not Check Your Weight for 30 Days

The whole30 is not only about the weight loss but it offers other lifelong health benefits. So, do not take your body measurements and stand on the scale time and again.

4. Don't Consider it Hard

There are many things that are hard in life, like giving birth to a baby, fighting a lethal disease, losing someone special, etc. These are the ACTUAL hard things in life, but following a whole30 diet is not hard at all. Stop considering it hard. It is just for 30 days and for the sake of your good health, don't make any excuse not to complete the challenge. You have done harder things in your life than this challenge.

5. Learn to Say No

When you are taking this challenge, learn to say "No" to all kinds of foods that are not the part of your whole30 diet. Don't make the parties, picnics and occasions an excuse to deviate from your diet plan. You are big and wise enough to refuse and select the options you have.

6. Do not Even Think About Slipping

When you are taking whole30 challenge, focus your mind on the diet and the reward that you will get after a month. So, do not consider slipping from the plan even an option. Eating something unhealthy is always a choice, so don't portray it as a slip or an accident. Commit to the challenge for the entire 30 days with all your will and might. Do not fail yourself before initiating the plan. You might want to quit the diet at every step, but think about the consequences and motivate yourself to move forward with full zeal and zest. Tell yourself time and again that you can do it.

7. Put in Your Continuous Efforts

When you are taking the whole30 challenge, you will have to face some other challenges too, like meal planning, explaining your program to others, grocery shopping, dining out and dealing with a lot of pressure and stress. You have been equipped with many advices, tools and resources, but you will have to take responsibility for your own plan. So, now you have to put in constant efforts to complete the challenge, getting rid of all the hurdles yourself.

Introduction to Crock-Pot

Everyone has a busy and hectic routine these days and no one has enough time to cook really good food on daily basis. But, then the crock-pots were invented and everyone praised their wonders. Cooking delicious and nutritious meals in less time and much convenient way was never this easy. Crock-pot is actually a brand name for a slow cooker. The crock-pot cooks food even when you are not in the kitchen and turns off automatically without burning the food.

If you have a family of four, then 3-quarts crock-pot works fine; whereas, 6-quarts would work well for larger families. The crock-pot has a removable inner pot that can be used for serving. Slow cooker is all about cooking at low temperature which allows most of the nutrients to remain in the food. A large variety of foods can be cooked in a crock-pot.

The Benefits of Using a Crock-Pot

There are numerous benefits of using the slow cooking technique in a crock-pot. Some of the benefits are as follows:

1. Saves Time

Crock-pots come in handy and are very easy to use. The preparation usually takes one step in which you have to put all the ingredients at once and start the pot. This saves a lot of time as to when you have to add things in different steps. It also cuts down on cleanup time.

2. Tenderizes Meats Properly

As the crock-pot takes a long time to cook at low temperature, the meat is tenderized properly even if the cuts on the meat are not too deep.

3. Uses Less Electricity

The crock-pot is cost-effective as it uses less electricity than an electric oven.

4. Reduces the Temptation of Ordering Take-out

The temptation to eat the foods from restaurants is eliminated when you cook food in a crock-pot. The food cooked in the crock-pot is very healthy, nutritious and tasty as compared to the outside food.

5. Does not Heat up the Kitchen

Making delicious foods in the crock-pot, like soups in winter, gives out aroma which is very welcoming. The plus point of the crock-pot is that it does not heat up the kitchen as the ovens do.

6. Cooks Flavorful Foods

Slow cooking in a crock-pot carries out the aroma and flavor in foods. As the cooking is slow at low temperature, so the nutritional value and taste of the foods are enhanced.

7. Cleaned up Easily

Due to the low temperature, the scorching foods do not stick to the bottom of the pot, thus, making it easier to clean the pot.

8. Used Conveniently

Unattended cooking is facilitated for many hours for the crock-pot. You do not have to worry about the food burning as it turns off automatically once the food is cooked.

What are Some Tips on How to Best Use My Crock-Pot?

If you want to make the best use of your crock-pot, you will have to follow some basic safety rules and tips, which are as follows:

1. Before using a crock-pot, spray the inside of the stoneware with nonstick cooking spray or rub with oil before using it. This will allow easy cleanup.
2. Keep in mind not to fill more than two-third and less than half full of the

crock-pot. The safety, cooking time and quality of the food are affected by cooking either too much or too little food.
3. Whenever you cook the vegetables and meat combined, put the vegetables in the slow cooker first because the vegetables cook slower than poultry and meat. Transfer the meat on top of the vegetables and then pour the liquids like water, sauce or broth.
4. For the first hour, set your crock-pot on high and afterwards, switch the heat setting to low in order finish cooking.
5. If you are cooking grains, like rice or pasta, add them at the end of the cooking process, otherwise they will become mushy. It is a useful tip to cook them separately or put them at the end just before serving.
6. In order to avoid curdling, add cream, cheese and milk during the last hour.
7. You cannot put the frozen meat directly in the crock-pot. You must defrost the meat and poultry in the fridge before cooking it in the crock-pot.
8. When you convert a non-slow cooker recipe for crock-pot use, you might lessen the liquids by one-third to one-

half because the liquids do not boil away in a crock-pot.
9. If you remove the lid of the crock-pot time and again while cooking, the cooking time is slowed down by 15 – 20 minutes. So, keep the lid of the pot in place while cooking.
10. A few vegetables are very soft, like zucchini, mushrooms and tomatoes. These must be added to the crock-pot during the last hour before serving.

Whole30 Crock-Pot Meat Recipes

Crock-Pot Turkey Breast

Serving: 5

Preparation Time: 15 minutes

Cook Time: 7 hours

Ingredients

- 2 pounds turkey breast
- 1 large onion
- 1 cup homemade chicken broth
- 3 garlic cloves
- Salt, to taste

How to

1. Season the turkey breast with salt and add to the crock-pot.
2. Put the remaining ingredients in the pot and set the crock-pot on Low.
3. Cook for about 7 hours and dish out.

Nutritional Information (Per Serving)

Calories: 211

Fat: 3.3g

Carbohydrates: 11.2g

Protein: 32.4g

Crock-Pot Orange Chicken

Serving: 6

Preparation Time: 10 minutes

Cook Time: 7 hours

Ingredients

- 2 pounds boneless chicken breasts
- 2 tablespoons lemon juice
- 2 teaspoons fresh orange peel, finely grated
- ½ cup orange juice
- Salt and pepper, to taste

How to

1. Season the chicken breasts with salt and pepper.
2. Put the seasoned chicken, lemon juice, orange juice and orange peel in the crock-pot.
3. Set the crock-pot on Low and cook for about 7 hours.
4. Dish out and serve.

Nutritional Information (Per Serving)

Calories: 298

Fat: 11.3g

Carbohydrates: 2.4g

Protein: 43.9g

Whole30 Savory Tater Tot

Serving: 8

Preparation Time: 15 minutes

Cook Time: 9 hours

Ingredients

- 2 pounds lean ground beef
- 24 ounces frozen potato rounds
- ½ onion, chopped
- ½ cup homemade bone broth
- 4 tablespoons ghee

How to

1. Add beef and ghee in a crock-pot.
2. Layer with diced onions and pour the bone broth in the pot.
3. Top with potato tater tots and set the crock-pot on Low.
4. Cook for about 9 hours and dish out.

Nutritional Information (Per Serving)

Calories: 520

Fat: 19.7g

Carbohydrates: 3.7g

Protein: 77.1g

Whole30 Chili Lime Turkey

Serving: 4

Preparation Time: 15 minutes

Cook Time: 7 hours

Ingredients

- 1½ pounds turkey thighs
- 1 small onion, diced
- 4 garlic cloves, minced
- ½ teaspoon dried parsley
- ½ tablespoon lime juice
- 1 tablespoon ghee
- ½ cup homemade chicken broth
- ½ teaspoon paprika
- Salt, to taste

How to

1. Season the turkey thighs with salt, paprika and parsley.
2. Add the seasoned thighs and rest of the ingredients in the crock-pot.
3. Set the crock-pot on Low and cook for about 7 hours.
4. Dish out and serve hot.

Nutritional Information (Per Serving)

Calories: 635

Fat: 12g

Carbohydrates: 3.3g

Protein: 71.6g

Whole30 Beef and Cabbage Stew

Serving: 8

Preparation Time: 15 minutes

Cook Time: 9 hours

Ingredients

- 2 pounds beef stew meat, trimmed and cubed
- 5 cups green cabbage, chopped
- 4 garlic cloves, minced
- 1 cup homemade beef broth
- 1 large onion, chopped
- 4 fresh tomatoes, chopped finely
- ¼ cup fresh parsley, chopped
- Salt and freshly ground black pepper, to taste

How To

1. Season the beef with salt and black pepper.
2. Place the onion, cabbage and garlic in the bottom of a large crock-pot.
3. Top with beef and then tomatoes.
4. Stir in the broth and set the crock-pot on Low.
5. Cover and cook for about 9 hours.
6. Garnish with fresh parsley and serve.

Nutritional Information (Per Serving)

Calories: 248

Fat: 7.4g

Carbohydrates: 7.4g

Protein: 36.5g

Crock-Pot Beef Steak

Serving: 5

Preparation Time: 10 minutes

Cook Time: 8 hours

Ingredients

- 2 pounds beef top sirloin steaks
- 1 teaspoon garlic powder
- 2 cloves garlic, minced
- ¼ cup ghee
- Salt and pepper to taste

How to

1. Season the beef sirloin steaks with garlic powder, salt and pepper.
2. Add the seasoned beef, garlic cloves and ghee in the crock-pot.
3. Set the crock-pot on Low and cook for about 8 hours.
4. Dish out and serve.

Nutritional Information (Per Serving)

Calories: 431

Fat: 21.5g

Carbohydrates: 0.8g

Protein: 55.2g

Whole30 Colorful Lamb

Serving: 10
Preparation Time: 15 minutes
Cook Time: 8 hours
Ingredients

- 2 pounds grass-fed boneless lamb, trimmed
- 6 garlic cloves, minced
- 1 tablespoon ghee
- 1 small green bell pepper, seeded and sliced into ½-inch thick strips
- 1 small yellow bell pepper, seeded and sliced into ½-inch thick strips
- 1 small red bell pepper, seeded and sliced into ½-inch thick strips
- 2 cups tomatoes, chopped finely
- 1 cup water
- Salt and black pepper, to taste

How to

1. Season the lamb with salt and pepper.

2. Put the seasoned lamb in the crock-pot and add all the ingredients in it.
3. Set the crock-pot on Low, cover and cook for about 8 hours.
4. Dish out in a platter and serve.

Nutritional Information (Per Serving)

Calories: 432

Fat: 34.7g

Carbohydrates: 6.2g

Protein: 25.2g

Crock-Pot Irish Stew

Serving: 6

Preparation Time: 15 minutes

Cook Time: 8 hours

Ingredients

- 6 lamb shoulder chops, cubed
- 6 large onions, sliced into thin rounds
- 3 cups water
- 3 tablespoons ghee
- 8 large carrots, chunked
- 2 sprig thymes
- Salt and black pepper, to taste

How to

1. Season the lamb chops with salt and black pepper.
2. In the crock-pot, put the ghee and onions.
3. Cook for 2 minutes and add rest of the ingredients.
4. Add the seasoned chops and set the crock-pot on Low.
5. Cook for about 8 hours and dish out.

Nutritional Information (Per Serving)

Calories: 326

Fat: 15.5g

Carbohydrates: 23.7g

Protein: 24.5g

Crock-Pot Special Leg of Lamb

Serving: 6

Preparation Time: 10 minutes

Cook Time: 8 hours

Ingredients

- 1 (2 pound) boneless leg of lamb
- 2 tablespoons ghee
- 1 tablespoon lemon juice
- ¼ cup chicken broth
- ½ tablespoon fresh rosemary, minced

- 1 teaspoon lemon zest, grated freshly
- ½ teaspoon ground cumin
- 1 teaspoon red pepper flakes, crushed
- 1 tablespoon fresh thyme, minced
- Salt and freshly ground black pepper, to taste

How To

1. Mix together ghee, herbs, garlic, spices and lemon zest in a bowl.
2. Rub the lamb with ghee mixture and transfer leg of lamb in a crock-pot.
3. Squeeze lemon juice and pour broth on the top.
4. Set the crock-pot on Low and cook for about 8 hours.

Nutritional Information (Per Serving)

Calories: 325

Fat: 15.6g

Carbohydrates: 0.9g

Protein: 42.8g

Crock-Pot Jamaican Jerk Pork Roast

Serving: 6

Preparation Time: 20 minutes

Cook Time: 8 hours

Ingredients

- 2 pounds pork shoulder
- 1 tablespoon ghee
- ¼ cup Jamaican jerk spice blend
- ¼ cup beef broth

How to

1. Marinate the pork in ghee and Jamaican jerk spice blend for 10 minutes.
2. Add the marinated pork and beef broth in the crock-pot.
3. Set the crock-pot on Low and cook for about 8 hours.
4. Dish out and serve hot.

Nutritional Information (Per Serving)

Calories: 462

Fat: 34.5g

Carbohydrates: 0g

Protein: 35.4g

Herbed Carrots Pork

Serving: 8
Preparation Time: 10 minutes
Cook Time: 9 hours
Ingredients

- 2 pound boneless pork shoulder roast
- 1 teaspoon dried oregano, crushed
- 1 tablespoon red pepper flakes, crushed
- 1 large onion, sliced thinly
- 1 teaspoon dried basil, crushed
- 1 teaspoon dried thyme, crushed
- 4 medium carrots, peeled and sliced lengthwise
- Salt and freshly ground black pepper, to taste

How To

1. Season the pork shoulder with dried herbs, salt and black pepper.
2. Transfer the pork in a bowl and keep aside for at least 3-4 hours.
3. Place carrots and onion in the bottom of a large crock-pot and sprinkle with salt and pepper.
4. Transfer the pork shoulder over carrots.
5. Set the slow cooker on Low and cook for about 8 hours.

Nutritional Information (Per Serving)

Calories: 354

Fat: 24.4g

Carbohydrates: 5.3g

Protein: 27g

Crock-Pot Beef Brisket

Serving: 6

Preparation Time: 10 minutes

Cook Time: 9 hours

Ingredients

- 2 pounds beef brisket
- 1 tablespoon ghee
- 2 small garlic cloves, minced
- ¼ cup beef broth
- 1 small onion, sliced
- ¼ teaspoon red pepper flakes, crushed
- ½ teaspoon ground cumin
- Salt and freshly ground black pepper, to taste

How To

1. Mix well all the ingredients in a large crockpot.
2. Set the crock-pot on Low, cover and cook for about 6 hours.
3. Uncover the crock-pot and transfer the brisket onto a cutting board.
4. Slice with a sharp knife and cut into desired slices to serve.

Nutritional Information (Per Serving)

Calories: 308

Fat: 11.7g

Carbohydrates: 1.6g

Protein: 46.3g

Whole Roasted Chicken

Serving: 4

Preparation Time: 10 minutes

Cook Time: 8 hours

Ingredients

- 1 (2-pound) whole chicken, cleaned, pat dried
- 1 carrot, peeled, cut into pieces
- 1 small onion, chopped
- 3 whole garlic cloves, peeled
- 1 celery stalk, chopped
- 1 tablespoon Herbs de Provence
- 2 tablespoons fresh lemon juice
- Salt and freshly ground black pepper, to taste

How to

1. Stuff the chicken cavity with garlic cloves and season with salt, pepper and herbs de Provence.
2. Place the vegetables in the bottom of a crock-pot and transfer the chicken on it.
3. Squeeze the lemon juice and set the crock-pot on Low.
4. Cover and cook for about 8 hours.

Nutritional Information (Per Serving)

Calories: 544

Fat: 17.3g

Carbohydrates: 23.7g

Protein: 69g

Crock-Pot Turkey Meatballs

Serving: 6

Preparation Time: 15 minutes

Cook Time: 8 hours 15 minutes

Ingredients

- 1 pound ground turkey
- 1 teaspoon garlic, minced
- 1 tablespoon olive oil
- ½ teaspoon red pepper flakes, crushed
- ½ teaspoon ground cumin
- 2 tablespoons fresh cilantro, minced
- 12-ounce tomatoes, peeled and crushed
- Salt, to taste

How To

1. Add all the ingredients in a bowl except tomatoes and mix until well combined.
2. Make desired sized balls from mixture.
3. Put tomatoes in a crock-pot and add the meat balls.
4. Cook on low for 8 hours.

Nutrition Values (Per Serving)

Calories: 180

Fat: 1.7g

Carbohydrates: 2.5g

Protein: 21.3g

Whole30 Pork Carnitas

Serving: 4

Preparation Time: 10 minutes

Cook Time: 8 hours

Ingredients

- 2 pounds bone-in pork shoulder
- 1 tablespoon ghee
- ¼ teaspoon dried oregano
- ½ teaspoon ground cumin
- ½ teaspoon garlic powder
- 1 orange, juiced
- 1 onion, chopped
- Salt and black pepper, to taste

How to

1. Season the pork with dried oregano, ground cumin, garlic powder, salt and pepper.
2. Put the seasoned pork, ghee, onion and orange in the crock-pot.
3. Set the crock-pot on Low and cook for about 8 hours.
4. Dish out and serve.

Nutritional Information (Per Serving)

Calories: 645

Fat: 49.5g

Carbohydrates: 8.4g

Protein: 39g

Whole30 Crock-Pot Seafood Recipes

Crock-Pot Scallion Salmon

Serving: 8

Preparation Time: 10 minutes

Cook Time: 2 hours

Ingredients

- 8 (6-ounce) salmon fillets
- 4 teaspoons ghee, divided
- 2 cups scallion, chopped
- 1/8 teaspoon ground cinnamon
- 1 tablespoon garlic powder
- 1 teaspoon red pepper flakes, crushed
- 2 tablespoons fresh lemon juice
- Salt and black pepper, to taste

How to

1. Season the salmon fillets with garlic powder, red pepper flakes, salt and black pepper.
2. Put the seasoned salmon fillets and rest of the ingredients in the crock-pot.
3. Set the crock-pot on Low and cook for about 2 hours.
4. Dish out and serve in a platter.

Nutritional Information (Per Serving)

Calories: 257

Fat: 12.8g

Carbohydrates: 2.8g

Protein: 33.7g

Whole30 Crock-Pot Cod Curry

Serving: 8

Preparation Time: 10 minutes

Cook Time: 3 hours

Ingredients

- 3 tablespoons ghee
- 1½ pounds frozen cod fillets
- 2 cups tomatoes
- 2 garlic cloves, minced
- 3 large carrots, peeled and chopped
- 2 cups water
- 3 cups fresh kale, trimmed and chopped
- 2 medium onions, chopped finely
- 3 tablespoons fresh parsley, chopped
- Salt and freshly ground black pepper, to taste

How to

1. Put the ghee in the crock-pot and add cod fillets.
2. Stir for 2 minutes and add rest of the ingredients.
3. Set the crock-pot on Low and cook for about 3 hours.

4. Dish out and serve in a platter.

Nutritional Information (Per Serving)

Calories: 337

Fat: 7.7g

Carbohydrates: 10g

Protein: 57.5g

Whole30 Tangy Cod Fillets

Serving: 6

Preparation Time: 15 minutes

Cook Time: 2.5 hours

Ingredients

- 2 pounds salmon fillet, cut into small pieces
- 2 cups homemade chicken broth
- 2 tablespoons ghee
- 3 teaspoons garlic, minced
- 6 tablespoons fresh lemon juice
- 2 teaspoons fresh lemon zest, grated finely
- Salt and freshly ground black pepper, to taste

How to

1. Mix all the ingredients in the crock-pot and set the crock-pot on Low.
2. Cook for about 2 hours and dish out.
3. Serve with boiled vegetables.

Nutritional Information (Per Serving)

Calories: 256

Fat: 14.2g

Carbohydrates: 31.2g

Protein: 27.6g

Rosemary Cod Fillets

Serving: 6

Preparation Time: 10 minutes

Cook Time: 2.5 hours

Ingredients

- 2 pounds cod fillets
- ¼ cup ghee
- 2 garlic cloves, minced
- 2 cups water
- 4 tablespoons fresh lemon juice
- 1 teaspoon dried oregano
- 4 lemon slices
- 4 fresh rosemary sprigs
- Salt and freshly ground black pepper, to taste

How to

1. Mix lemon juice, oil, garlic, oregano, salt and black pepper in a bowl.
2. Transfer the cod fillets in the crock-pot and pour the prepared mixture over it.
3. Put the lemon slices and rosemary sprigs on the fillets.
4. Set the crock-pot on Low and cook for about 2.5 hours.
5. Dish out and serve in a platter.

Nutritional Information (Per Serving)

Calories: 205

Fat: 10.1g

Carbohydrates: 1.7g

Protein: 27.3g

Crock-Pot Energetic Salmon Fillets

Serving: 4

Preparation Time: 10 minutes

Cook Time: 2 hours

Ingredients

- 4 (4-ounce) salmon fillets
- 2 garlic cloves, minced
- 2 tablespoons fresh rosemary, chopped
- ½ pound tomatoes, halved

- 1 tablespoon ghee
- Salt and freshly ground black pepper, to taste

How to

1. Put rosemary and half of tomatoes at the bottom of the crock-pot.
2. Transfer the remaining tomatoes and salmon fillets on top in a layer.
3. Season with garlic, salt and black pepper, and drizzle the ghee.
4. Set the crock-pot on Low and cook for about 2 hours.
5. Dish out and serve in a platter.

Nutritional Information (Per Serving)

Calories: 196

Fat: 10.6g

Carbohydrates: 3.8g

Protein: 22.7g

Whole30 Foolproof Mahi-Mahi Fillets

Serving: 4

Preparation Time: 15 minutes

Cook Time: 1.5 hours

Ingredients

- 1 pound mahi-mahi fillets
- 3 lemon slices
- ½ teaspoon garlic powder
- 1 tablespoon ghee
- 2 fresh dill sprigs
- ½ cup water
- Salt and black pepper, to taste

How to

1. Season the mahi-mahi fillets with garlic powder, salt and black pepper.
2. Top the fillets with lemon slices, dill sprigs and ghee.
3. Put the mahi-mahi fillets in the crock-pot and set the crock-pot on Low.
4. Cook for about 1.5 hours and dish out.

Nutritional Information (Per Serving)

Calories: 122

Fat: 3.2g

Carbohydrates: 1g

Protein: 21.3g

Crock-Pot Whole30 Cauliflower Fish

Serving: 6

Preparation Time: 15 minutes

Cook Time: 3 hours

Ingredients

- 2 pounds salmon fillets
- 2 tablespoons ghee
- 1 cup cauliflower
- 1 small onion, quartered
- 1 teaspoon garlic powder
- 3 garlic cloves, peeled
- Salt and black pepper, to taste

How to

1. Put the ghee in the crock-pot and add salmon fillets.
2. Stir for 3 minutes and add the rest of the ingredients.
3. Set the crock-pot on Low and cook for about 3 hours.
4. Dish out and serve in a platter.

Nutritional Information (Per Serving)

Calories: 250

Fat: 13.6g

Carbohydrates: 2.8g

Protein: 30g

Crock-Pot Super Easy Mahi-Mahi

Serving: 4

Preparation Time: 15 minutes

Cook Time: 2 hours

Ingredients

- 1 pound mahi-mahi fillets
- 2 lemon slices
- 2 teaspoons fresh lemon juice
- Salt and freshly ground black pepper, to taste

How to

1. Season the mahi-mahi fillets with salt and pepper.
2. Put the seasoned mahi-mahi fillets in the crock-pot and set the crock-pot on Low.
3. Cook for about 2 hours and dish out.

Nutritional Information (Per Serving)

Calories: 92

Fat: 0g

Carbohydrates: 0.4g

Protein: 21.1g

Crock-Pot Quick Lobster

Serving: 2

Preparation Time: 10 minutes

Cook Time: 3 hours

Ingredients

- 1½ pounds lobster tails, cut in half
- 1 teaspoon salt
- 1 teaspoon turmeric powder
- 1 cup water
- 1½ tablespoons ghee

How to

1. Put all the ingredients in the crock-pot.
2. Set the crock-pot on Low and cook for about 3 hours.
3. Dish out and serve in a platter.

Nutritional Information (Per Serving)

Calories: 491

Fat: 20.7g

Carbohydrates: 0.4g

Protein: 71.3g

Crock-Pot Salmon with Vegetables

Serving: 8

Preparation Time: 10 minutes

Cook Time: 2.5 hours

Ingredients

- 2 pounds salmon fillets
- 4 cups fresh broccoli
- 4 cups spinach
- 10 asparagus stalks

- 1 tablespoon ghee
- 1 tablespoon lemon juice
- 2 tablespoons red pepper flakes
- Salt and pepper, to taste

How to

1. Put all the vegetables in the crock-pot.
2. Combine olive oil, lemon juice, red pepper flakes, salt and pepper in a bowl.
3. Dredge the fish in this mixture and place the fish in the crock-pot.
4. Set the crock-pot on Low and cook for about 2.5 hours.
5. Dish out and serve in a platter.

Nutritional Information (Per Serving)

Calories: 221

Fat: 9.3g

Carbohydrates: 10.9g

Protein: 27.6g

Whole30 Lemon Salmon

Serving: 6

Preparation Time: 10 minutes

Cook Time: 1 hour

Ingredients

- 2 pounds salmon fillets
- 1 shallot, sliced thinly
- 4 tablespoons lemon juice
- 1½ cups water
- 1 lemon, sliced thinly
- Salt and freshly ground black pepper, to taste

How to

1. Mix together all ingredients except salmon fillets in a crock-pot.

2. Transfer salmon fillets on top and set the crock-pot on Low.

3. Cover and cook for about 60 minutes.

4. Dish out and serve.

Nutritional Information (Per Serving)

Calories: 206

Fat: 9.4g

Carbohydrates: 1.4g

Protein: 29.6g

Crock-Pot Moroccan Fish

Serving: 6

Preparation Time: 10 minutes

Cook Time: 2 hours

Ingredients

- 2 pounds salmon fillets
- ¾ teaspoon ghee
- 2 garlic cloves, crushed
- ¾ pound cherry tomatoes, crushed slightly
- ¾ teaspoon red pepper flakes, crushed
- ¾ teaspoon dried oregano, crushed
- ¾ tablespoon fresh basil leaves, torn
- Salt, to taste

How to

1. Put the ghee in the crock-pot and add salmon fillets.
2. Stir for 2 minutes and add rest of the ingredients.
3. Set the crock-pot on Low and cook for about 2 hours.
4. Dish out and serve in a platter.

Nutritional Information (Per Serving)

Calories: 218

Fat: 10g

Carbohydrates: 2.8g

Protein: 30g

Crock-Pot Mahi-Mahi with Carrots

Serving: 6

Preparation Time: 10 minutes

Cook Time: 3 hours

Ingredients

- 2 pounds mahi-mahi fillet, cut into 4 pieces
- ½ cup carrots
- 2 garlic cloves, minced
- 2 teaspoons ground cumin
- 2 tablespoons red chili powder
- 2 cups water
- Salt and freshly ground black pepper, to taste

How to

1. Mix together all ingredients except mahi-mahi and carrots in a small bowl.
2. Dredge mahi-mahi pieces in the spice mixture.
3. Transfer mahi-mahi and carrots in the crock-pot.
4. Set the crock-pot on Low and cook for about 3 hours.
5. Dish out and serve in a platter.

Nutritional Information (Per Serving)

Calories: 136

Fat: 0.6g

Carbohydrates: 2.9g

Protein: 28.7g

Crock-Pot Fish Curry

Serving: 6

Preparation Time: 10 minutes

Cook Time: 1 hour

Ingredients
- 2 pounds salmon fillets, cut into bite sized pieces
- 1 small onion, chopped
- 2 tablespoons curry powder
- 2 cups tomatoes, chopped
- 2 garlic cloves, minced
- 1 teaspoon red chili powder
- 1 tablespoon ghee
- 2 teaspoons ground coriander
- 1 tablespoon fresh lemon juice
- 2 teaspoons ground cumin

How to
1. Put all the ingredients in the crock-pot except the salmon fillets.
2. Put the salmon fillets on the top.
3. Set the crock-pot on Low and cook for about 1 hour.

4. Dish out and serve hot.

Nutritional Information (Per Serving)

Calories: 247

Fat: 12.1g

Carbohydrates: 5.6g

Protein: 30.5g

Crock-Pot Delicious Mussels

Serving: 2
Preparation Time: 10 minutes
Cook Time: 2.5 hours
Ingredients

- 1 pound mussels, cleaned and de-bearded
- 1 small onion, chopped
- 1 garlic clove, minced
- ½ cup homemade chicken broth
- ½ teaspoon dried rosemary, crushed
- 1 tablespoon ghee
- 1 tablespoon fresh lemon juice
- Salt and freshly ground black pepper, to taste

How to

1. Put the ghee in the crock-pot and add onions.
2. Sauté for 3 minutes and add mussels.
3. Stir for 3 more minutes and add the remaining ingredients.
4. Set the crock-pot on Low and cook for about 2.5 hours.
5. Dish out and serve in a platter.

Nutritional Information (Per Serving)

Calories: 280

Fat: 12g

Carbohydrates: 12.7g

Protein: 28.8g

Whole30 Crock-Pot Soup Recipes

Crock-Pot Mexican Beef Soup

Serving: 4
Preparation Time: 10 minutes
Cook Time: 8 hours
Ingredients

- 1 pound grass-fed lean ground beef
- 1 cup tomatoes, diced
- 3 garlic cloves, minced
- 1½ teaspoons ground cumin
- 1 teaspoon ghee
- 4 cups homemade beef broth
- 2 tablespoons chili powder
- Salt and black pepper, to taste
- 1 cup baby spinach

How to

1. Put all the ingredients in the crock-pot and set the crock-pot on Low.
2. Cover and cook for about 6 hours.
3. Dish out and serve with garnishing of baby spinach.

Nutritional Information (Per Serving)

Calories: 262

Fat: 13g

Carbohydrates: 6.2g

Protein: 27.5g

Whole30 Crock-Pot Chicken Veggie Soup

Serving: 6

Preparation Time: 10 minutes

Cook Time: 4 hours

Ingredients

- 2 pounds grass-fed cooked chicken, shredded
- 3 tablespoons ghee
- 5 large carrots, peeled and chopped
- 8 cups homemade chicken broth
- 3 cups fresh kale, trimmed and chopped
- 1 teaspoon dried thyme, crushed
- 1 cup water
- 5 celery stalks, chopped
- 1 teaspoon dried oregano, crushed
- 2 small onions, chopped
- Salt and freshly ground black pepper, to taste

How to

1. Put the ghee in the crock-pot and add onions and garlic.
2. Cook for about 5 minutes and add in the rest of the ingredients.
3. Set the crock-pot on Low and cook for about 4 hours.

Nutritional Information (Per Serving)

Calories: 292

Fat: 9.7g

Carbohydrates: 10.1g

Protein: 39.1g

Crock-Pot Vegetable Pork Soup

Serving: 4

Preparation Time: 10 minutes

Cook Time: 7 hours

Ingredients

- 1 pound pork meat
- 4 cups homemade chicken broth
- ½ teaspoon garlic powder
- 8-ounce frozen mix veggies (yellow onion, bell pepper)
- 1 teaspoon chili powder
- ½ cup green chilies, chopped
- 1 cup diced tomatoes
- ½ cup fresh cilantro, chopped
- Salt and black pepper, to taste

How to

1. Put all the ingredients in the crock-pot except cilantro.
2. Set the crock-pot on Low and cook for 3 hours.
3. Open the crock-pot and take out the pork.

4. Shred the pork meat and put it back in the crock-pot.
5. Set the crock-pot on Low and cook for another 4 hours.
6. Dish out and garnish with cilantro.

Nutritional Information (Per Serving)

Calories: 449

Fat: 36.2g

Carbohydrates: 9.9g

Protein: 20.3g

Whole30 Veggie Soup

Serving: 6

Preparation Time: 10 minutes

Cook Time: 4 hours

Ingredients

- 6 cups homemade vegetable broth
- 1 teaspoon dried thyme, crushed
- 4 cups cauliflower, chopped
- 1 tablespoon garlic, minced
- 1 pound fresh Baby Bella mushrooms, chopped
- 1 small onion, chopped
- 2 teaspoons ghee

How to

1. Put the ghee in the crock-pot and add onion and garlic.
2. Add in the rest of the ingredients and set the crock-pot on Low.
3. Cover and cook for about 4 hours.

Nutritional Information (Per Serving)

Calories: 59

Fat: 0.3g

Carbohydrates: 12g

Protein: 3.5g

Crock-Pot Green Soup

Serving: 4

Preparation Time: 10 minutes

Cook Time: 6 hours

Ingredients

- 1 pound chicken
- 2 cups homemade chicken broth
- 3 carrots, sliced
- 1 bunch kale, chopped
- 1 cup mushrooms, sliced
- 1 cup water

How to

1. Add the chicken, carrots and mushrooms in the crock-pot.
2. Blend the kale with the chicken broth and pour it in the pot.
3. Set the crock-pot on Low and cook for about 6 hours.
4. Dish out and serve hot.

Nutritional Information (Per Serving)

Calories: 221

Fat: 4.2g

Carbohydrates: 7.3g

Protein: 36.7g

Whole30 Zucchini Ginger Soup

Serving: 6

Preparation Time: 10 minutes

Cook Time: 4 hours 5 minutes

Ingredients

- 2 pounds medium zucchini, chopped
- 1 tablespoon ghee
- 4 garlic cloves, minced
- 2 teaspoons ground ginger
- 4 cups homemade chicken broth
- 1 small onion, chopped
- Salt and black pepper, to taste

How to

1. Put the ghee in the crock-pot and add onions.
2. Sauté for 3 minutes and add garlic and ground ginger.
3. Stir for about 2 minutes and add zucchini, broth, salt and black pepper.
4. Set the crock-pot on Low and cook for another 4 hours.
5. Dish out and garnish with parsley.

Nutritional Information (Per Serving)

Calories: 78

Fat: 3.4g

Carbohydrates: 7.9g

Protein: 5.4g

Crock-Pot Savory Carrot Soup

Serving: 6

Preparation Time: 10 minutes

Cook Time: 4 hours

Ingredients

- ½ pound carrots, peeled and chopped
- ¼ teaspoon dried parsley, crushed
- 3 cups homemade chicken broth
- 1 garlic clove, minced

- ¼ teaspoon dried basil, crushed
- 1 tablespoon vinegar
- 2 tablespoons fresh cilantro, chopped
- 1 small yellow onion, chopped
- 2 tablespoons ghee
- 4 tablespoons coconut aminos
- Salt and black pepper, to taste

How to

1. Put the ghee in the crock-pot and add onion.
2. Stir in the rest of the ingredients and set the crock-pot on Low.
3. Cover and cook for about 4 hours.

Nutritional Information (Per Serving)

Calories: 88

Fat: 4.9g

Carbohydrates: 7.5g

Protein: 2.9g

Crock-Pot Turkey Thai Soup

Serving: 4

Preparation Time: 15 minutes

Cook Time: 7 hours

Ingredients

- 1 pound turkey breast, cooked and chopped
- 1 cup fresh green beans
- 2 tablespoons red curry paste
- 1 lime, cut into wedges
- 2 cups chicken broth
- 1 red bell pepper, chopped
- 1 medium onion, sliced
- 2 tablespoons red curry paste
- ½ cup baby spinach
- 1 tablespoon fresh ginger grated

How to

1. Put all the ingredients in the crock-pot and set the crock-pot on Low.
2. Cover and cook for about 7 hours.
3. Dish out and garnish with baby spinach.

Nutritional Information (Per Serving)

Calories: 303

Fat: 7.5g

Carbohydrates: 27.2g

Protein: 25.8g

Crock-Pot Curried Broccoli Soup

Serving: 6

Preparation Time: 10 minutes

Cook Time: 4 hours 5 minutes

Ingredients

- 1½ pounds broccoli florets
- 2 tablespoons ghee
- 1 large onion, chopped
- 4 cups bone broth
- 4 leeks, thinly sliced
- 3 shallots, roughly chopped
- ½ apple, peeled and diced small
- 1 tablespoon curry powder
- Salt and pepper, to taste

How to

1. Put the ghee in the crock-pot and add onion, leeks and shallots.
2. Cook for 5 minutes and then add rest of the ingredients.
3. Set the crock-pot on Low and cook for about 4 hours.
4. Dish out and serve in a bowl.

Nutritional Information (Per Serving)

Calories: 299

Fat: 6g

Carbohydrates: 42.4g

Protein: 26.5g

Crock-Pot Special Chicken Soup

Serving: 4

Preparation Time: 15 minutes

Cook Time: 2 hours 10 minutes

Ingredients

- 1 pound organic chicken
- 1 tablespoon ghee
- 1 shallot, chopped
- 3 garlic cloves, chopped
- 1 teaspoon paprika
- 1 teaspoon thyme
- 1 carrot, peeled & chopped
- ½ cup parsley
- 5 cups water
- 1 medium onion, chopped
- 1 bunch dill
- 1 bunch kale, broken into 1-inch pieces

How to

1. Heat ghee over medium heat in a crock-pot and add onion, shallot and garlic.
2. Cook for 10 minutes and add the chicken.
3. Stir in the paprika, thyme, salt and pepper.
4. Put the carrots, dill, kale and parsley in the pot.
5. Add the water to the pot and set the crock-pot on Low.

6. Cover and cook for about 2 hours.

Nutritional Information (Per Serving)

Calories: 235

Fat: 6.8g

Carbohydrates: 8.1g

Protein: 34.4g

Crock-Pot Chicken Tortilla Whole30 Soup

Serving: 4
Preparation Time: 15 minutes
Cook Time: 4 hours
Ingredients

- 2 pounds chicken breasts
- 1 tablespoon garlic powder
- 1 teaspoon chili powder
- 3 cloves garlic, diced
- 1 jalepeno pepper, de-seeded and finely diced
- 2 cups homemade chicken broth
- ¼ cup lime juice
- 2 plaintain chips

- 2 tablespoons cumin
- 1 tablespoon cayenne pepper
- 1 yellow onion, diced
- 1 red bell pepper, diced
- 1 can diced tomatoes with green chiles
- Salt and pepper, to taste

How to

1. Put the chicken breasts, garlic powder, cumin, chili powder and cayenne pepper in the crock-pot.
2. Cook on Low for 4 hours.
3. After about 2 hours, take out the chicken, shred it and put it back in the crock-pot.
4. Stir in the garlic, onion, bell pepper, diced tomatoes, chicken broth and jalapeno peppers.
5. Cook for another 2 hours and stir in the lime before serving.

Nutritional Information (Per Serving)

Calories: 385

Fat: 14.8g

Carbohydrates: 14.3g

Protein: 47.3g

Crock-Pot Yummy Lamb Soup

Serving: 9

Preparation Time: 10 minutes

Cook Time: 7 hours 15 minutes

Ingredients

- 1½ pounds grass-fed ground lamb meat
- 1½ tablespoon garlic, minced
- 1½ pound fresh green beans, trimmed and cut into 1-inch pieces
- 1½ tablespoon ghee
- 1 small yellow onion, chopped
- 3 teaspoons dried thyme, crushed
- 5 cups fresh tomatoes, chopped finely
- 6 cups homemade beef broth
- Salt and freshly ground black pepper, to taste

How to

1. Put the ghee in the crock-pot and add beef.
2. Cook for 3 minutes while continuously stirring.
3. Add rest of the ingredients and set the crock-pot on Low.
4. Cover and cook for another 7 hours.
5. Dish out and serve hot.

Nutritional Information (Per Serving)

Calories: 289

Fat: 12.4g

Carbohydrates: 26.4g

Protein: 22.4g

Whole30 Vegetable Turkey Soup

Serving: 6
Preparation Time: 15 minutes
Cook Time: 6 hours
Ingredients

- 1½ pounds lean ground turkey
- 3 cups carrots, peeled and shredded
- 6 cups homemade chicken broth
- 2 teaspoons ground ginger
- 2 tablespoons ghee
- 2 small onions, chopped
- 1 head cabbage, chopped
- 4 tablespoons vinegar
- Salt and black pepper, to taste

How to

1. Put all the ingredients in the crock-pot and set the crock-pot on Low.
2. Cover and cook for about 6 hours.
3. Dish out and serve hot.

Nutritional Information (Per Serving)

Calories: 142

Fat: 5.8g

Carbohydrates: 15.9g

Protein: 7.2g

Crock-Pot Omega-3 Salmon Soup

Serving: 4

Preparation Time: 10 minutes

Cook Time: 4 hours 5 minutes

Ingredients

- 1 pound salmon fillets
- 1 cup carrots, peeled and chopped
- ½ cup onion, chopped
- 3 cups homemade chicken broth
- 2 tablespoons ghee
- ½ cup celery stalk, chopped
- 1 cup cauliflower, chopped
- 1 cup water
- ½ cup kale
- ½ cup fresh parsley, chopped
- Salt and black pepper, to taste

How to

1. Put the ghee in the crock-pot and add the onions.
2. Sauté for 3 minutes and add rest of the ingredients except parsley.

3. Set the crock-pot on Low and cook for another 4 hours.
4. Dish out and garnish with parsley.

Nutritional Information (Per Serving)

Calories: 267

Fat: 14.5g

Carbohydrates: 7.8g

Protein: 27.1g

Whole30 Red Curry Soup

Serving: 4

Preparation Time: 10 minutes

Cook Time: 5 hours

Ingredients

- 1 pound chicken, shredded
- 1 cup full fat coconut milk
- 3½ tablespoons red curry paste
- ½ cup cooked spaghetti squash
- ½ cup mushrooms
- 1 can fire-roasted diced tomatoes
- 1 teaspoon powdered ginger
- ½ cup grilled peppers
- ½ cup spinach leaves

- Salt and black pepper, to taste

How to

1. Add all the ingredients in the crock-pot except cooked spaghetti squash.
2. Set the crock-pot on Low and cook for about 5 hours.
3. Dish out and pour over cooked spaghetti squash.

Nutritional Information (Per Serving)

Calories: 274

Fat: 11.2g

Carbohydrates: 5.8g

Protein: 34g

Whole30 Crock-Pot Desserts and Snacks Recipes

Crock-Pot Chicken Wings

Serving: 4
Preparation Time: 10 minutes
Cook Time: 4 hours 30 minutes
Ingredients

- ½ cup Frank's Wing Sauce
- 1 pound chicken wings, trimmed of fat
- 1 tablespoon salt
- ½ cup whole30 barbecue sauce
- ½ cup water

How to

1. Season the wings with salt and transfer the wings in the crock-pot.
2. Stir in the barbecue sauce, Frank's Wing Sauce and water in the crock-pot.
3. Set the crock-pot on Low and cook for about 4 hours and 30 minutes.
4. Dish out in a platter.

Nutritional Information (Per Serving)

Calories: 263

Fat: 8.5g

Carbohydrates: 11.5g

Protein: 32.8g

Crock-Pot Spiced Nuts

Serving: 6

Preparation Time: 5 minutes

Cook Time: 3 hours

Ingredients

- 1 cup almonds
- 1 cup cashews
- 1 cup pecans
- ½ teaspoon garlic powder
- ½ teaspoon black pepper
- ¼ teaspoon cayenne pepper
- 1½ teaspoon chili powder
- ½ teaspoon cumin
- ½ teaspoon sea salt
- 1 tablespoon ghee

How to

1. Put the ghee, almonds, cashews and pecans in the crock-pot.
2. Season with all the spices and stir gently.
3. Set the crock-pot on Low and cook for about 3 hours.
4. Dish out and serve.

Nutritional Information (Per Serving)

Calories: 267

Fat: 22.7g

Carbohydrates: 12.9g

Protein: 7.5g

Crock-Pot Whole30 Nut Porridge

Serving: 2

Preparation Time: 10 minutes

Cook Time: 4 hours

Ingredients

- ½ cup raw, unsalted cashews
- ½ cup unsweetened dried coconut shreds
- ½ cup pecan halves
- 2 teaspoons coconut oil, melted
- ½ apple, peeled
- ¼ cup pepitas, shelled
- 1 cup water

How to

1. Add coconut shreds, pecans, cashews, apple and pepitas in a food processor and blend well.
2. Transfer the mixture into the crock-pot and add ghee and water.
3. Set the crock-pot on Low and cook for about 4 hours.
4. Dish out and serve hot.

Nutritional Information (Per Serving)

Calories: 351

Fat: 24.8g

Carbohydrates: 29.3g

Protein: 5.9g

Crock-Pot Cajun Spiced Pecans

Serving: 5

Preparation Time: 5 minutes

Cook Time: 2 hours 30 minutes

Ingredients

- 1 pound pecan halves
- 1 tablespoon chili powder
- 1 teaspoon dried basil
- 1 teaspoon dried thyme
- ¼ teaspoon garlic powder
- 2 tablespoons ghee
- 1 teaspoon dried oregano
- ½ teaspoon cayenne pepper
- Salt, to taste

How to

1. Put all the ingredients in the slow cooker.
2. Set the crock-pot on High and cook for about 20 minutes.
3. Turn the crock-pot on Low and cook for about 2 hours.
4. Dish out the nuts and allow them to cool.

Nutritional Information (Per Serving)

Calories: 92

Fat: 9.4g

Carbohydrates: 2.3g

Protein: 0.7g

Crock-Pot Butternut Squash

Serving: 2

Preparation Time: 1 minute

Cook Time: 6 hours

Ingredients

- 1 whole butternut squash, washed
- Salt and black pepper, to taste

How to

1. Season the butternut squash with salt and pepper.
2. Put the seasoned whole butternut squash in the crock-pot and set the crock-pot on Low.
3. Cover and cook for about 6 hours.
4. When cool, cut in half and scoop out seeds.

Nutritional Information (Per Serving)

Calories: 90

Fat: 0.8g

Carbohydrates: 16.5g

Protein: 3g

Crock-Pot Roasted Spicy Olives

Serving: 4

Preparation Time: 10 minutes

Cook Time: 4 hours

Ingredients

- 3 cups mixed green and black olives
- 2 tangerines
- 3 cloves of garlic
- 2 tablespoons vinegar
- 1 inch piece of turmeric, finely grated
- 1 fresh red chili, thinly sliced
- 3 sprigs rosemary
- 2 tablespoons ghee

How to

1. Put all the ingredients except the tangerines in the crock-pot.
2. Squeeze the tangerines over all the ingredients.
3. Set the crock-pot on Low and cook for about 4 hours.
4. Dish out in a platter.

Nutritional Information (Per Serving)

Calories: 111

Fat: 10.3g

Carbohydrates: 5.3g

Protein: 0.6g

Crock-Pot Baked Potatoes

Serving: 3

Preparation Time: 10 minutes

Cook Time: 8 hours

Ingredients

- 3 large potatoes, well-scrubbed
- Salt, to taste
- 1 tablespoon ghee
- 3 sheets aluminum foil

How to

1. Rub the potatoes with ghee and salt.
2. Wrap the potatoes tightly in the aluminum foil.
3. Transfer the potatoes in the crock-pot.
4. Set the crock-pot on Low and cook for about 8 hours.

Nutritional Information (Per Serving)

Calories: 292

Fat: 4.6g

Carbohydrates: 58g

Protein: 6.2g

Crock-Pot Garlic Lemon Scallops

Serving: 6

Preparation Time: 5 minutes

Cook Time: 2 hours 10 minutes

Ingredients

- 2 pounds large scallops
- 3 tablespoons ghee
- 2 tablespoons fresh lemon juice
- 3 tablespoons garlic, minced
- Salt and pepper, to taste

How to

1. Put the ghee in the crock-pot and add garlic.
2. Cook for 3 minutes and add scallops.
3. Stir in the lemon juice, salt and pepper.
4. Set the crock-pot on Low and cook for about 2 hours.
5. Dish out in a platter.

Nutritional Information (Per Serving)

Calories: 313

Fat: 8.2g

Carbohydrates: 10.4g

Protein: 48.4g

Whole30 Cooked Guacamole

Serving: 4

Preparation Time: 10 minutes

Cook Time: 2 hours

Ingredients

- 1 small onion, finely diced
- ¼ cup cilantro, chopped
- 3 tablespoons lemon juice
- 3 avocados, peeled and diced
- 2 jalapenos, finely diced
- 2 tablespoons ghee
- Salt and black pepper, to taste

How to

1. Mix the onion, cilantro, lemon juice, avocados, jalapenos and ghee.
2. Put the mixture in the crock-pot and season with salt and pepper.
3. Set the crock-pot on Low and cook for about 2 hours.
4. Dish out in a platter.

Nutritional Information (Per Serving)

Calories: 376

Fat: 35.9g

Carbohydrates: 15.3g

Protein: 3.3g

Pumpkin Butter

Serving: 4

Preparation Time: 15 minutes

Cook Time: 4 hours 30 minutes

Ingredients

- 2 (15-oz) cans of pumpkin
- 1 cup coconut aminos
- 1 vanilla bean, scraped
- 1 pinch black pepper
- 1 tablespoon cinnamon
- ½ cup ruby port
- 1 pinch salt
- 1 pinch cayenne

How to

1. Stir together pumpkin, coconut aminos, vanilla bean, ruby port, salt, cayenne and pepper in your crock-pot.
2. Set the crock-pot on High and cook for 3 hours 30 minutes.
3. Open the lid and add cinnamon.
4. Let the mixture simmer for about 1 hour without the lid.

Nutritional Information (Per Serving)

Calories: 187

Fat: 1.5g

Carbohydrates: 35.1g

Protein: 3.2g

Crock-Pot Whole30 Applesauce

Serving: 5

Preparation Time: 15 minutes

Cook Time: 4 hours

Ingredients

- 2 large honey crisp apples, peeled
- 7 gala apples, peeled
- 5 golden delicious apples, peeled
- 1 teaspoon ground cinnamon
- 2 tablespoons fresh lemon juice
- ¼ teaspoon ground nutmeg

How to

1. Toss the apples with cinnamon, lemon juice and nutmeg.
2. Put the apples in the crock-pot and set the crock-pot on Low.
3. Cook for about 4 hours.
4. Pour all the mixture in an immersion blender and blend well.

Nutritional Information (Per Serving)

Calories: 217

Fat: 1.2g

Carbohydrates: 53.8g

Protein: 1g

Crock-Pot Almond Butter Banana

Serving: 4

Preparation Time: 10 minutes

Cook Time: 3 hours

Ingredients

- 4 medium-sized bananas
- 2 teaspoons cinnamon
- 4 tablespoons almond butter

How to

1. Cut the bananas from the middle and stuff with almond butter.
2. Sprinkle with cinnamon and put the bananas in the crock-pot.
3. Set the crock-pot on Low and cook for 3 hours.

Nutritional Information (Per Serving)

Calories: 206

Fat: 9.4g

Carbohydrates: 30.9g

Protein: 4.7g

Crock-Pot Grain Free Berry Cobbler

Serving: 4

Preparation Time: 10 minutes

Cook Time: 3 hours

Ingredients

- ½ cup almond flour
- ¼ cup coconut flour
- 1 cup coconut aminos
- ¼ teaspoon ground cinnamon
- 1 tablespoon ghee
- 2 pinches of salt
- 1 cup fresh or frozen blueberries, thawed
- 1 cup fresh or frozen raspberries, thawed

How to

1. Mix together almond flour, coconut flour, ghee, coconut aminos and ground cinnamon.
2. Pour the mixture into a baking mold and put the mold in the crock-pot.
3. Put the berries gently over the top and cook on Low for 3 hours.
4. Allow it to cool before serving.

Nutritional Information (Per Serving)

Calories: 288

Fat: 10.8g

Carbohydrates: 41.7g

Protein: 4.7g

Spinach Mushroom Treat

Serving: 3

Preparation Time: 10 minutes

Cook Time: 4 hours 6 minutes

Ingredients

- 1 pound fresh mushrooms, sliced
- 1 cup spinach
- 1 cup homemade chicken broth
- 2 garlic cloves, minced
- 2 tablespoons fresh thyme, chopped
- Freshly ground black pepper, to taste
- 1 medium onion, chopped
- 2 tablespoons ghee
- 2 tablespoons fresh cilantro, chopped

How to

1. Pour ghee in the crock-pot and select "Sauté".
2. Add the onion and cook for about 4 minutes.
3. Add garlic and cook for about 2 minutes.
4. Transfer in the spinach, mushrooms, broth and thyme.

5. Set the crock-pot on Low and cook for about 4 hours.
6. Garnish with cilantro and serve.

Nutritional Information (Per Serving)

Calories: 145

Fat: 9.6g

Carbohydrates: 10.9g

Protein: 7.4g

Crock-Pot Apple Butter

Serving: 3

Preparation Time: 5 minutes

Cook Time: 3 hours

Ingredients

- 3 pounds apples
- 1 tablespoon apple cider vinegar
- ¼ teaspoon nutmeg
- 2 teaspoons cinnamon
- 1 teaspoon ghee

How to

1. Mix all the ingredients in the crock-pot and stir well.
2. Set the crock-pot on Low and cook for about 3 hours.

3. Pour all the mixture in an immersion blender and blend well.

Nutritional Information (Per Serving)

Calories: 134

Fat: 1.9g

Carbohydrates: 32.2g

Protein: 0.7g

Crock-Pot Stuffed Apples with Figs

Serving: 4

Preparation Time: 10 minutes

Cook Time: 2 hours

Ingredients

- 4 apples with the center core hollowed out
- 4 dried figs
- ½ teaspoon fresh ginger
- ¼ cup of coconut aminos
- ¼ cup pecans, chopped
- ¼ teaspoon nutmeg
- 1 teaspoon lemon zest
- 1 tablespoon fresh lemon juice
- ¼ teaspoon salt
- ½ teaspoon cinnamon
- ½ teaspoon orange zest

- 1 tablespoon ghee
- ½ cup water

How to

1. Mix all the ingredients together except the apples.
2. Stuff this mixture in the core of the apples.
3. Put the water in the slow cooker and then add the stuffed apples.
4. Set the crock-pot on Low and cook for about 2 hours.
5. Dish out and serve.

Nutritional Information (Per Serving)

Calories: 180

Fat: 4.1g

Carbohydrates: 38g

Protein: 0.8g

Whole30 Crock-Pot Apple Cinnamon Quinoa

Serving: 4

Preparation Time: 10 minutes

Cook Time: 8 hours

Ingredients

- 1 cup quinoa, rinsed
- 1 teaspoon vanilla extract
- ½ cup unsweetened apple sauce
- 2 teaspoon ground cinnamon
- 2 cups water
- 1 small apple, peeled and cut in to small cubes
- 1 pinch salt

How to

1. Mix together all the ingredients in your crock-pot.
2. Set the crock-pot on Low and cook for 8 hours.
3. Dish out and serve as breakfast.

Nutritional Information (Per Serving)

Calories: 204

Fat: 2.7g

Carbohydrates: 39.5g

Protein: 6.3g

Whole30 Crock-Pot Appetizer Recipes

Crock-Pot Buffalo Wings

Serving: 6
Preparation Time: 10 minutes
Cook Time: 4 hours
Ingredients

- 2 pounds chicken wings
- ¾ teaspoon salt
- 4 tablespoons ghee
- 2 tablespoons avocado oil
- 2 teaspoons garlic powder
- ½ cup Frank's Original Red Hot

How to

1. Season the wings with salt, oil and garlic powder.
2. Add the seasoned wings in the crock-pot and pour in the ghee, avocado oil and Frank's Original Red Hot.
3. Set the crock-pot on Low and cook for about 4 hours.

Nutritional Information (Per Serving)

Calories: 372

Fat: 20.3g

Carbohydrates: 1.1g

Protein: 44g

Crock-Pot Avocado Wedges

Serving: 3

Preparation Time: 15 minutes

Cook Time: 3 hours

Ingredients

- 2 ripe avocados
- 2 egg whites
- 2 tablespoons olive oil
- 4 tablespoons coconut flour
- ¼ teaspoon sea salt
- ¼ teaspoon freshly ground black pepper

How to

1. Mix together coconut flour, salt and pepper.
2. Whisk egg whites in a bowl.
3. Cut the avocados in the wedges and dip in the egg whites.
4. Dredge the avocados in the dry mixture.
5. Put the olive oil in a crock-pot and add avocados.
6. Set the crock-pot on Low and cook for about 3 hours.

Nutritional Information (Per Serving)

Calories: 228

Fat: 19.3g

Carbohydrates: 11.8g

Protein: 4.9g

Crock-Pot Spicy Pickles

Serving: 4

Preparation Time: 15 minutes

Cook Time: 3 hours

Ingredients

- 8 pickle slices
- 1 tablespoon ghee
- ½ cup almond flour
- 1 teaspoon cumin
- ½ teaspoon chili powder
- ½ teaspoon red pepper flakes
- 1 egg white, beaten
- 1 tablespoon sriracha

How to

1. Whisk egg whites and sriracha in a bowl.
2. Mix together almond flour, cumin, chili powder and red pepper flakes.

3. Dip the pickle slices in the egg mixture.
4. Dredge the pickle slices in the dry mixture.
5. Put the ghee and pickle slices in the crock-pot and set it on Low.
6. Cook for about 4 hours and serve.

Nutritional Information (Per Serving)

Calories: 125

Fat: 10.1g

Carbohydrates: 4.7g

Protein: 4.1g

Whole30 Sweet Potato Bacon Tots

Serving: 5

Preparation Time: 20 minutes

Cook Time: 3 hours

Ingredients

- 1 large sweet potato
- 5 strips crispy bacon, chopped
- ½ teaspoon onion powder
- ½ cup cassava flour
- 3 tablespoons avocado oil

- Salt and pepper, to taste

How to

1. Put the sweet potato and some water in a crock-pot and set the crock-pot on Low.
2. Cook for about 1 hour and open the lid.
3. Mix the sweet potato, bacon, onion powder, salt, black pepper and cassava flour until fully combined.
4. Roll into small tots shape and put it in the crock-pot.
5. Set the crock-pot on Low and cook for about 2 hours.

Nutritional Information (Per Serving)

Calories: 181

Fat: 9.2g

Carbohydrates: 16.4g

Protein: 8.1g

Crock-Pot Carrot Fries

Serving: 4

Preparation Time: 5 minutes

Cook Time: 3 hours

Ingredients

- 8 large carrots
- 1 teaspoon garlic powder
- 1 cup fresh cilantro
- 1 tablespoon avocado oil
- Salt and pepper, to taste

How to

1. Mix avocado oil, garlic powder and fresh cilantro.
2. Cut carrots in matchsticks and dredge in the above mixture.
3. Put the carrots in the crock-pot and set to Low.
4. Cook for about 3 hours and serve with the dip of your choice.

Nutritional Information (Per Serving)

Calories: 67

Fat: 0.5g

Carbohydrates: 15g

Protein: 1.4g

Whole30 Brussels Sprouts with Bacon Garlic Aioli

Serving: 5

Preparation Time: 20 minutes

Cook Time: 4 hours

Ingredients

- 1 pound Brussels sprouts, washed and trimmed
- 2 tablespoons avocado oil
- Salt and pepper, to taste
- ½ cup mayonnaise
- 2 garlic cloves, minced finely
- 2 strips of cooked bacon, finely chopped
- 2 teaspoons lemon juice
- 1 teaspoon dried thyme

How to

1. Season the Brussels sprouts with salt and pepper.
2. Mix mayonnaise, garlic cloves, cooked bacon, lemon juice and dried thyme to make aioli.
3. Put the oil in the crock-pot and add the sprouts.
4. Set the crock-pot on Low and cook for about 4 hours.
5. Serve with the bacon garlic aioli.

Nutritional Information (Per Serving)

Calories: 181

Fat: 12.5g

Carbohydrates: 14.8g

Protein: 5.1g

Bacon Compote and Caramelized Onion on Sweet Potato

Serving: 4

Preparation Time: 15 minutes

Cook Time: 5 hours

Ingredients

- 3 sweet onions, cut in half and thinly sliced
- 3 dates, pitted & chopped
- 5 slices of thick sliced bacon
- 1 tablespoon chopped fresh Rosemary
- 1 tablespoon ghee
- 1 sweet potato, sliced
- 1 tablespoon avocado oil
- Salt and pepper, to taste

How to

1. Put ghee in a crock-pot and add rest of the ingredients except sweet potato slices and avocado oil.
2. Set the crock-pot on Low and cook for about 3 hours.
3. Remove the mixture from the pot and add avocado oil and sweet potato slices.

4. Set the crock-pot on Low and cook for about 2 hours.
5. In a plate, put the sweet potato slices and top with the bacon and onion mixture.

Nutritional Information (Per Serving)

Calories: 199

Fat: 11.4g

Carbohydrates: 19g

Protein: 5.5g

Crock-Pot Whole30 Zucchini

Serving: 4

Preparation Time: 10 minutes

Cook Time: 3 hours

Ingredients

- 2 medium-length zucchini, cut into ½ inch round slices
- 1 teaspoon dried dill
- 1 teaspoon paprika
- 1 egg
- 2 tablespoons coconut oil
- 3 tablespoons coconut flour
- 2 tablespoons almond milk
- Sea salt, to taste

How to

1. Whisk egg and almond milk together in a small bowl.

2. Mix the salt, paprika, dried dill and coconut flour.

3. Dip the slices in the egg mixture.

4. Dredge the zucchini slices in the dry mixture.

5. Put the coconut oil in a crock-pot and add the zucchini slices.

6. Set the crock-pot on Low and cook for about 3 hours.

Nutritional Information (Per Serving)

Calories: 126

Fat: 10.4g

Carbohydrates: 6.8g

Protein: 3.2g

Whole30 Cobb-Style Potato

Serving: 3
Preparation Time: 10 minutes
Cook Time: 4 hours
Ingredients

- 1 large potato, cut into slices
- ½ avocado, cut into small cubes
- 4 hard-boiled eggs, sliced lengthwise
- 2 pieces of whole30 approved bacon, cooked and crumbled

How to

1. Put the potato slices in a crock-pot and set the crock-pot on Low.

2. Cook for about 4 hours and transfer the potato slices in a plate.

3. Top each with an egg slice and add cubed avocado on the top.

4. Divide bacon crumbles evenly and serve hot.

Nutritional Information (Per Serving)

Calories: 257

Fat: 13.5g

Carbohydrates: 25g

Protein: 10.9g

Whole30 Teriyaki Poppers

Serving: 4

Preparation Time: 10 minutes

Cook Time: 3 hours

Ingredients

- 1 small head cauliflower, chopped into bite-sized pieces
- ½ cup pineapple, pureed
- 1 tablespoon sesame seed oil
- ¼ cup coconut flour
- ¼ cup coconut aminos
- 1 teaspoon ground ginger

How to

1. Mix coconut flour and cauliflower in a bowl and stir to coat.
2. Mix together pineapple puree, sesame seed oil, coconut aminos and ground ginger.
3. Coat the cauliflower in the mixture and put it in crock-pot.
4. Set the crock-pot on Low and cook for about 3 hours.

Nutritional Information (Per Serving)

Calories: 88

Fat: 4.2g

Carbohydrates: 11.2g

Protein: 1.2g

Whole30 Crock-Pot Beverages Recipes

Whole30 Berry Kombucha Beverage

Serving: 2
Preparation Time: 10 minutes
Cook Time: 1 hour
Ingredients
- 1 (12-oz) sparkling water
- ½ cup frozen mixed berries
- 1 (16-oz) kombucha bottle

How to
1. Put all the ingredients in the crock-pot.
2. Set the crock-pot on Low and cook for about 1 hour.
3. Pour out the mixture and serve.

Nutritional Information (Per Serving)

Calories: 180

Fat: 0.1g

Carbohydrates: 44.3g

Protein: 0.3g

Crock-Pot Berry Lemonade Tea

Serving: 6

Preparation Time: 10 minutes

Cook Time: 3 hours

Ingredients

- 6 tea bags
- 3 cups natural lemonade
- 6-ounce frozen mixed berries
- 4 cups water
- 2 lemons, sliced

How to

1. Put all the ingredients in the crock-pot except lemons.
2. Set the crock-pot on Low and cook for about 3 hours.
3. Strain the mixture in the cups and put the lemon slices.

Nutritional Information (Per Serving)

Calories: 87

Fat: 0.2g

Carbohydrates: 21.2g

Protein: 0.4g

Whole30 Red Cherry Cider

Serving: 4

Preparation Time: 15 minutes

Cook Time: 4 hours

Ingredients

- 2 cups apple juice
- 4 cups cherry juice
- 2 (1-inch) cinnamon sticks

How to

1. Put apple juice, cherry juice and cinnamon sticks in the crock-pot.
2. Set the crock-pot on Low and cook for about 4 hours.
3. Strain out the mixture and serve hot.

Nutritional Information (Per Serving)

Calories: 96

Fat: 0.1g

Carbohydrates: 23.8g

Protein: 0.3g

Crock-Pot Spiced Peachy Cider

Serving: 8

Preparation Time: 15 minutes

Cook Time: 4 hours

Ingredients

- 8 cups peach nectar
- 1 teaspoon ground ginger
- ½ teaspoon ground nutmeg
- 4 cups apple juice
- ½ teaspoon ground cinnamon
- 8 fresh orange slices (½-inch thick)

How to

1. Put all the ingredients in the crock-pot except orange slices.
2. Set the crock-pot on Low and cook for about 4 hours.
3. Strain out the mixture in 8 cups and place each orange slice in each cup.

Nutritional Information (Per Serving)

Calories: 179

Fat: 0.8g

Carbohydrates: 43.7g

Protein: 2.8g

Crock-Pot Red Hot Punch

Serving: 4

Preparation Time: 15 minutes

Cook Time: 4 hours

Ingredients

- 1 cup hot brewed tea
- 1 cup apple juice
- 1 cup pineapple juice
- 1 cup orange juice
- 4 tablespoons Frank's Red Hot
- 4 mint leaves

How to

1. Put all the ingredients in the crock-pot.
2. Set the crock-pot on Low and cook for about 3 hours 30 minutes.
3. Strain out the mixture and serve hot.

Nutritional Information (Per Serving)

Calories: 99

Fat: 0.4g

Carbohydrates: 23g

Protein: 1.1g

Crock-Pot Spiced Pear Cider

Serving: 4

Preparation Time: 5 minutes

Cook Time: 3 hours

Ingredients

- 8 whole allspice
- 2 (3-inch) cinnamon sticks
- 1 cup pear nectar
- 4 whole cloves
- 3 cups unsweetened pear juice

How to

1. Put all the ingredients in the crock-pot except apple and orange slices.
2. Set the crock-pot on Low and cook for about 3 hours.
3. Strain out the mixture and serve with apple and orange slices.

Nutritional Information (Per Serving)

Calories: 108

Fat: 0.8g

Carbohydrates: 27.9g

Protein: 0.6g

Crock-Pot Spiked Cider

Serving: 4

Preparation Time: 10 minutes

Cook Time: 6 hours

Ingredients

- 6 apples, sliced
- 1 orange, sliced
- ½ tsp nutmeg
- 1 cup fresh cranberries
- 3-4 cinnamon sticks
- 6 cups water

How to

1. Add apples, cranberries, organic cassava syrup, cinnamon sticks, nutmeg and orange in the crock-pot.
2. Stir in the water and set the crock-pot on Low.
3. Cook for 6 hours and strain the mixture using mesh strainer.

Nutritional Information (Per Serving)

Calories: 216

Fat: 0.8g

Carbohydrates: 55.6g

Protein: 1.4g

Crock-Pot Spiced Apple Orange Cider

Serving: 6

Preparation Time: 10 minutes

Cook Time: 3 hours

Ingredients

- 6 cups apple juice
- 2 tablespoons lemon juice
- 2 cups orange juice
- 4 tablespoons whole allspice
- 1 teaspoon cinnamon powder
- Apple slices
- Orange slices

How to

1. Put all the ingredients in the crock-pot except apple and orange slices.
2. Set the crock-pot on Low and cook for about 4 hours.
3. Strain out the mixture and serve with apple and orange slices.

Nutritional Information (Per Serving)

Calories: 192

Fat: 1g

Carbohydrates: 47.3g

Protein: 1.4g

Whole30 Swedish Glögg

Serving: 4

Preparation Time: 10 minutes

Cook Time: 4 hours

Ingredients

- 1 cup orange juice
- 1 (½-inch) piece fresh ginger
- 3 whole cloves
- 2 cardamom pods, opened
- 3 tablespoons orange zest
- 1 cinnamon stick
- 3 whole allspice
- 1 vanilla bean

How to

1. Put all the ingredients in the crock-pot.
2. Set the crock-pot on Low and cook for about 4 hours.
3. Strain out the mixture and serve.

Nutritional Information (Per Serving)

Calories: 72

Fat: 1.6g

Carbohydrates: 14.6g

Protein: 1.6g

Whole30 Homemade Lemonade

Serving: 4

Preparation Time: 12 minutes

Cook Time: 4 hours

Ingredients

- 2 cups water
- 2 cups fresh lemon juice
- 5 mint leaves
- 2 (1-inch) cinnamon sticks

How to

1. Put all the ingredients in the crock-pot.
2. Set the crock-pot on Low and cook for about 4 hours.
3. Strain out the mixture and serve hot.

Nutritional Information (Per Serving)

Calories: 38

Fat: 1.1g

Carbohydrates: 4.7g

Protein: 1.5g

Crock-Pot Hot Pomegranate Punch

Serving: 6

Preparation Time: 15 minutes

Cook Time: 2 hours

Ingredients

- 2 cups pomegranate juice
- 2 cups unsweetened apple juice
- 1 cup brewed tea
- 1 cup lemon juice
- 6 whole cloves
- 1 (1-inch) cinnamon stick

How to

1. Put all the ingredients in the crock-pot.
2. Set the crock-pot on Low and cook for about 2 hours.
3. Strain out the mixture and serve hot.

Nutritional Information (Per Serving)

Calories: 107

Fat: 0.8g

Carbohydrates: 24.6g

Protein: 0.5g

Whole30 Fruit Punch

Serving: 10

Preparation Time: 12 minutes

Cook Time: 3 hours 30 minutes

Ingredients

- 2 cups hot brewed tea
- 2 cups apple juice
- 2 cups cranberry juice
- 2 cups orange juice
- 1 cup apricot juice
- 1 cup lemon juice
- 6 whole cloves
- 1 (1-inch) cinnamon stick

How to

1. Put all the ingredients in the crock-pot.
2. Set the crock-pot on Low and cook for about 3 hours 30 minutes.
3. Strain out the mixture and serve hot.

Nutritional Information (Per Serving)

Calories: 81

Fat: 0.6g

Carbohydrates: 17.4g

Protein: 0.7g

Ginger Lemon Tea

Serving: 6

Preparation Time: 10 minutes

Cook Time: 4 hours

Ingredients

- 4 cups water
- 1 (2-inch) piece fresh ginger, peeled
- 1 cup fresh lemon juice
- 2 tablespoons ginger, chopped
- 2 tablespoons fenugreek seeds

How to

1. Put all the ingredients in the crock-pot.
2. Set the crock-pot on Low and cook for about 4 hours.
3. Strain out the mixture and serve.

Nutritional Information (Per Serving)

Calories: 34

Fat: 0.8g

Carbohydrates: 5.6g

Protein: 1.5g

Whole30 Hot Mulled Cider

Serving: 6

Preparation Time: 5 minutes

Cook Time: 4 hours

Ingredients

- 4 cups apple cider
- 2 tablespoons cinnamon powder
- 1 (1-inch) piece of ginger
- 1 cup apricot nectar
- 1 cup orange juice
- 1 teaspoon pumpkin pie spice
- 6 whole cloves
- 1 fresh orange, sliced

How to

1. Put all the ingredients in the crock-pot except apple and orange slices.
2. Set the crock-pot on Low and cook for about 4 hours.
3. Strain out the mixture and serve with apple and orange slices.

Nutritional Information (Per Serving)

Calories: 143

Fat: 0.8g

Carbohydrates: 34.9g

Protein: 1g

Crock-Pot Ginger Spiced Cider

Serving: 6

Preparation Time: 10 minutes

Cook Time: 3 hours

Ingredients

- 2 whole cloves
- 1 whole allspice
- 1 teaspoon fresh ginger
- 1 small apple, peeled
- 2 teaspoons orange zest
- 1 teaspoon cinnamon powder
- 6 cups apple cider
- ¼ teaspoon ground nutmeg

How to

1. Put all the ingredients in the crock-pot.
2. Set the crock-pot on Low and cook for about 3 hours.
3. Strain out the mixture and serve.

Nutritional Information (Per Serving)

Calories: 141

Fat: 0.6g

Carbohydrates: 35.2g

Protein: 0.4g

Conclusion

The whole30 challenge claims to reduce inflammation, aid weight loss and improve gut health. The followers of the whole30 diet must cook the most amounts of their meals from the scratch as there are many restrictions in this diet. If you want to commit to this healthy boost and want to still have a life, then you must try the above-mentioned recipes of whole30 crock-pot meals. Whether you are looking for delicious, clean recipes or following the whole30 program, these 87 remarkable dishes are definitely worth trying and are just what you need. With this cookbook, eating nutritious and healthy foods is not complicated at all. Making dinners out of whole food approved crock pot recipes is a breeze.

Each recipe in this book has been carefully constructed, verified and integrates only unprocessed, fresh meats, spices, herbs and vegetables. These recipes cover the entire range of food requirements from savory to sweet. These dishes are easy to make in the crock-pot and saves you a lot of time. It makes cooking preparation and cleanup much easier.

The crock-pot is such a convenient tool that cooks nutritious and delicious foods for you in your absence. You can dump all the ingredients in the crock-pot and forget about them for hours. The versatility of this whole30 crock-pot cookbook is depicted by the variety of food types it covers. You can find the wide diversity of beef, pork, lamb, poultry, snacks, desserts and beverages recipes that can be cooked very effortlessly in the crockpot. The crock-pot serves as your partner in motivating you at its level best to fulfill your whole30 challenge successfully. This book provides you with both the health and the taste.

www.ingramcontent.com/pod-product-compliance
Lightning Source LLC
Chambersburg PA
CBHW052207090526
44583CB00016BA/1784